THE NATURE CURE
AND DUODENAL ULCE

With digestive ailments becomin[g] [...] [c]ommonplace the author of this book has outlined [...] [...]se of drugless self-treatment for the gastric sufferer, giving clear instructions for the easy application of the commonsense methods described. Also included is sound dietetic advice for parents, enabling them to establish in their children the foundations of a healthy adulthood.

By the same author

HOW TO CURE CATARRHAL DEAFNESS AND HEAD
   NOISES
THE SUCCESSFUL TREATMENT OF CATARRH
THE NATURAL TREATMENT OF LIVER TROUBLES
NATURE CURE FOR RHEUMATIC AILMENTS
THE NATURE CURE TREATMENT OF VARICOSE VEINS
   AND ULCERS
NATURE CURE FOR HIGH BLOOD-PRESSURE
THE SUCCESSFUL TREATMENT OF HAIR DISORDERS

The Nature Cure Treatment of Gastric and Duodenal Ulcerations

J. Russell Sneddon N.D., M.B.N.O.A.

THORSONS PUBLISHERS LIMITED
Wellingborough, Northamptonshire

First published 1946
Ninth Impression 1972
Second Edition (revised and reset) 1975

ISBN 0 7225 0314 8

Typeset by Specialised Offset Services Ltd., Liverpool
and printed and bound by Weatherby Woolnough
Wellingborough, Northamptonshire

Contents

1.
Methods of Cure

A study of newspaper advertisements often gives a reliable clue to the most common ailments of the moment – digestive complaints especially provide lucrative investments for present-day patent medicine vendors. Following this, it has been found that approximately one person in every ten suffers from some form of digestive ailment and that the more serious forms, such as gastric and duodenal ulcerations, are daily becoming more numerous. These distressing and dangerous conditions now rank among the greatest scourges of modern times.

Such numerous patent medicine advertisements indicate that the ordinary allopathic treatment is not successful, because in this country medical services are cheap and, if successful, the sufferer need not seek the relatively expensive patent medicine. Therefore, it must be concluded that the percentage of cure by allopathic medicine in digestive ailments is not high. Normally the sufferer who relies on the patent medicines has previously tried the usual allopathic drugs, and so it would appear that this aspect of modern medicine stands in danger of passing from the physician to the chemist.

However, whether the medicine is supplied straight from the chemist or delivered on receipt of a medical prescription, the results are roughly the same: namely, temporary relief.

Soon the medicines lose their effect and resort must be made to stronger ones.

In fairness to the conscientious medical practitioner, who is one of the most hard working of men and who is actually doing his best to allay the suffering of mankind, it must be remembered that many practitioners try to impress upon the patient the danger of the alkaline medicine. Once he has done this, however, what more can he do? It must be left to the patient to decide whether he suffers the pain or takes the medicine. The doctor can do no more.

ALLOPATHIC LIMITATIONS
The limitations of allopathic medicine are definite and yet are surprisingly little understood by the layman, who has been taught from impressionable infancy that the doctor can cure anything physical. Certainly he can resort to diet, but the average doctor unfortunately is such a busy man that he cannot find the time to consider dietetic cures. He may well be interested in the possibility of cure by diet, but has probably never been able to make a deep study of it.

So, if the doctor resorts to diet, it is probably a patent diet like the patent medicine. It has been drafted out in thousands of sheets and the sufferer is included in the general classification as a gastric subject. His individual requirements are not studied in any way. He becomes one of the many.

The diet which is advocated is a non-irritating one composed of soft foods which contain little or no roughage, the idea being that the ulcerated and inflamed part of the bowel is soothed rather than irritated by the passage of food along its inner wall. In this respect the soft diet is seemingly successful and relief is often felt quite quickly, thus leading the patient to think that a cure has at last been found.

But cure is always a relative term, and subsequent findings prove the fallacy of quick results because the bland diet only soothes but never cures ulceration. Instead, it causes a mineral-deficient condition which is followed by more digestive tract inflammation and so results the very condition it is supposed to cure.

Nearly every patient received by Nature Cure practitioners has been on a bland diet eked out with alkaline medicines, and each and every one of these patients has the same story to tell of seeming cure and then gradual return of pain and sickness, accompanied in the latter instance by a nervous depression which has effects on the individual more deadly than the actual pain. That is another result of the bland diet. Due to its unbalanced character, it deprives the system of vital mineral salts essential to health, both mental and physical, and it is impossible to have a buoyant natural spirit in a minerally deficient system.

SURGICAL OPERATION

Until comparatively recently, surgical operation was generally regarded as the only correct treatment for gastric and upper bowel ulceration. It was the method which had the full support of all the orthodox practitioners, but not that of the less hide-bound members of the unorthodox branches of healing. These latter practitioners maintained that many cases did not require an operation but rather a complete change of diet and the stressing of simple rules of eating and drinking.

Now, with the passing of time, the success of the latter treatment has been tested, proved and recognized, and today ulceration is commonly regarded as a case for the dietitian and physician, not the surgeon, and medicinal and dietary treatment take the place of the knife.

No wise practitioner, however, implies that surgical interference is never necessary, because many cases of perforation require immediate operation if the leakage is acute and the peritoneal cavity is becoming inflamed. The skill of the surgeon can then save many lives, a factor recognized by every branch of the healing art.

But perforation of the digestive tract is usually the result of neglect on the part of the practitioner or patient and in almost every case can be prevented by attending to a few simple rules. Unfortunately these instructions are often overlooked by the practitioner or not obeyed by the patient, and the number of gastric perforations is rising yearly and operations become essential in all these cases. Once such an operation has been performed, a complete cure is always difficult due to the formation of scar tissue which takes place on healing.

GASTRIC TROUBLES ON THE INCREASE

In spite of the change in treatment of gastric complaints, the numbers of such sufferers are still increasing rapidly, so much so that a famous Glasgow practitioner recently remarked that gastric troubles are now as great a scourge as tuberculosis used to be in this country, and that training in food rules is essential to the cure.

This is a very enlightening remark, because it stresses what has been the finding of most unorthodox practitioners, namely, that the condition of the emotions, the tone of the physical body and the balancing of food are all important factors in these complaints. The best food, balanced in every respect, is harmful under conditions of emotional distress or when the body does not signify the need for food. These are factors which are not often brought out in the allopathic system of treating digestive ailments, mainly because the practitioner has not the time to spare on the individual patient.

NATURE CURE SYSTEM

In a large practice it is common to have many cases of ulcerations and I feel that this book on the subject, based on the findings of many cases, will be helpful to the sufferers of these complaints. It is written from the viewpoint of the Nature Cure system of healing and living, which is based upon the theory that the body will always try to heal and that any disease within reason can be cured by the positive vitality of the body itself. In Nature Cure no drugs or medicines are used because it is believed that these are at all times unnatural and even injurious to the system and may in themselves cause further ill-health.

The cure is brought about by corrective dieting, with the effort being directed towards natural elimination in addition to sufficient assimilation. Other methods of treatment include remedial exercises, water treatments and positive psychology. This may seem rather complicated to the beginner, but the opposite is actually the case; although certain little points may seem strange to the reader and student who has been brought up in a background which places all health matters within the realm of the allopathic practitioner.

HOME TREATMENT

An actual course of treatment has been arranged whereby the gastric sufferer can carry out the system in his or her own home. That this is not an ideal method is readily admitted, but the Nature Cure system is as yet not widely known, so it is not possible for everyone to get in touch with such practitioners. At the same time, if a practitioner is available, his services should be sought, even if for advice only, because it is always preferable to home treatment without personal supervision.

It will be natural for the reader to ask how long this course will take, but that is a very difficult question to answer, because it depends greatly on the healing vitality within the body and the amount of impurity in the tissues. Progress will depend greatly on these two factors and also upon the enthusiasm of the sufferer. But this I can say with confidence:

once you have undergone this system of treatment for a few weeks, there will come to you a feeling of progress, in many cases completely indefinable but nevertheless certain, and your enthusiasm will mount from that day. You will appreciate that you are on the road to health.

This does not mean that you will have no further set-backs – rather the reverse, because as healing proceeds, the body will continually dictate its demands and often these will be accompanied by pain, especially if they are not obeyed with alacrity. In this respect, pain, within limits, is healing and its signs should be obeyed, and with this obedience will come the feeling that the pain is never so intense and has changed in character. The need to control the discomfort by alkaline medicines will disappear and the rest of the body will benefit in consequence.

2.
Making a Start

One of the greatest difficulties experienced by the beginner in naturopathic dieting is that of deciding how the new foods should be introduced. In this I am not in agreement with many books on the subject, which lay down hard and fast diet sheets which should be commenced immediately without regard to after-effects. This is wrong because curative dieting to be effective must be accompanied by other measures which will retone the body in general and the stomach and bowels in particular. To treat the digestive system as a part completely separate from the rest of the body is absurd. It depends for its efficiency upon the blood and nerve flow and lymphatic drainage of the entire body and these are all factors essential to its well-being. Therefore when we set out to repair some organic weakness, we must at the same time institute measures which will bring the rest of the body into line, because one organ cannot fail in its duty without repercussion throughout the system.

Experience has proved that a wholesale dietetic change is too sudden for the delicate mechanism of the stomach and is often followed by an upset far greater than the original. It is very much better from every point of view not to change the diet but rather to reduce it in quantity. The patient must try to get an idea of the foods which agree with his constitution and keep to this limited diet in the beginning, thus keeping the inflammation under control until a stage of dietetic change is reached and new foods can be safely introduced.

THE DIARY

The best way to do this is to write a daily diary of each and every article of food taken at a meal, including liquids taken with the food. This should be entered on the left hand side of the paper and on the right side you should note your remarks, made some time afterwards, stating whether the meal agreed with you or not. Gradually it will become clear, over a period of two or three weeks, that certain foods or food mixtures do not suit your constitution. This should be rectified and after some time the suspected food should be tried again. If it does not agree on this occasion, it should be disgarded temporarily, or even permanently, as unsuitable for your chemical make-up.

If a diet is reached which does not seemingly disagree but which does not make you feel in perfect digestive health, it is common to find that the mixtures of solids and liquids are at fault, and you should then experiment with dry and 'wet' meals. This means that you should take all your meals completely dry when on the dry diet, taking liquid between meals and only when actually thirsty. The fluid diet, on the other hand, means that liquid may be taken immediately before or after the solid part of the meal. Careful application of these findings will leave you on a diet which, although it may be completely unbalanced and not health-giving from the Nature Cure standpoint, will keep the stomach and bowel in the quiescent state. Naturally, it will take a varying period (up to one month) to decide on such a diet, and then you can start to eliminate gradually the following foods and liquids which are definitely detrimental to physical health.

DETRIMENTAL FOODS AND LIQUIDS

Certain foods definitely do not agree in gastric complaints and therefore I am supplying a list of these to enable the reader to decide quickly the foods which are suspect. Here they are:

Fried and greasy foods: These are always difficult to digest and require very efficient stomach and liver action. They must be completely stopped in all cases of gastric distress, even if actual ulceration is not present.

Meat foods: These require a high amount of acid in the stomach for their digestion, and acid causes more pain and flatulence in the sensitive stomach. It is best, therefore, to reduce the meat ration slowly until it also is completely stopped in two or three weeks.

Fresh acid fruits: These include apples, oranges, pears, grapefruit, lemons, pineapples, strawberries, gooseberries and all berries. Although such fruits have an alkaline reaction in the normal stomach, it is most doubtful if this occurs in the abnormal one, and experience proves them harmful, at least at the beginning of the treatment. They will be advised during the later stages of the cure, in reduced amounts.

Condiments, preserves and sugar: Salt, sauces, vinegar, jam and sugar are all stomach irritants, spoiling the complete flavour of natural foods, and they too must be quickly reduced in quantity.

Tea, coffee, spirits and wines: In every case these liquids create an acid reaction in the stomach and should be reduced. Tea and coffee lovers will find this most difficult, and I would advise a gradual reduction rather than a complete stoppage, because soon the desire for such liquids will vanish and they may even become distasteful in certain cases. This is due to the fact that much of the desire for their stimulation comes from the wrong food mixtures being introduced into the diet and once this is corrected the desire for liquid of this description is lessened. This is a common finding of all Nature Cure practitioners although it is difficult to get certain patients to believe they will come to dislike their favourite beverage.

STICK TO THE DIET

Once you have checked your diet and found the one most suitable to you (because it varies with each individual), keep strictly to this food plan. You are not cured because you have no pain — you have only started 'stomach resting', an important factor in the cure. After this you have to balance the diet and introduce food which will enable real healing to take place.

In many cases the keeping of a diet chart will bring about fairly good results and yet an occasional meal will be followed by upset. Neither rhyme nor reason will appear at this stage to be accountable for this distress and the reader will have to study this book further for the answer. Such symptoms should be treated fairly vigorously with plenty of warm water and complete fasting until the appetite is again healthy. Never eat until you feel very hungry in these cases, and you have started the elimination of the cause. If you take food when the hunger is more apparent than real, the next upset will be more severe and difficult to remedy. Sickness, acidity and flatulence are definite signs that the body does not desire food. See that you obey such warnings!

There is one little point with regard to the taking of water during fasting. Usually warm water is wanted, and it appears efficient in most cases, but there are outstanding cases which benefit more from cold water. It is a case of trial and error.

That is the end of the first lesson and the reader will be inclined to think that the change has been rather drastic, but actually these foods and liquids which have been stopped are detrimental in this condition and no cure is possible when they are taken.

YOUR HEALING VITALITY

You may think, rather ruefully, that this start has been more of a reduction than anything else. With that I agree, but would add that it is not within the power of any other person to heal your body. You must do the healing yourself, and by reducing the harmful and unsuitable foods you are allowing your healing vitality to rise. In other words, you immediately start to get better when you stop poisoning yourself, and by decreasing the work done on needless digestion you are allowing the body to concentrate on the weakened parts of the system.

If you have been taking an alkaline medicine, the quantity should be curtailed until it is completely withheld. The natural reaction to this will be a slight increase in pain, which should be treated simply by sipping small amounts of whole milk. The other dietetic changes will soon render such pain bearable and the stoppage of the alkali will enable the kidneys to deal more quickly and efficiently with the impurities in the blood.

Again I would stress that you must think of the body as a whole. It is easy to fall into the habit of judging your health by the condition of your stomach. This course is directed at *whole health*, and you must consider it from that angle. Take your feelings collectively and you will soon find that everything reduces to its true perspective. This control of thought is a technique which must be acquired by every seeker after good health because it is a vital part of the conquest of disease. You must use it to give great value to the varying changes which betoken an increase in health and to belittle those which mean a loss of physical rhythm. By using thought and imagination in this way you are allowing the intelligence of your tissue cells to direct the processes of repair.

3.
The Rules of Eating

After the soothing diet has been established and the detrimental foods stopped, it would appear natural to start with other dietetic changes immediately, but in practice this is not so beneficial as a training in little, simple and seemingly unimportant factors of eating and drinking. This is one of the most important lessons in this course, and it must be studied minutely by all stomach sufferers if they wish to obtain the utmost benefit from the balanced diet which will be advocated in later chapters.

Food is eaten to supply materials for the various functions of the body, and to allow the eliminative function of the body to work normally. Most of us eat too much for all these purposes, and nearly all of us eat food at the wrong time. Natural hunger is the only sign of food requirement, but as it is a condition which is usually infrequently met with, the need arises for the laying down of certain rules which must be observed if health is to be regained and maintained.

NEVER EAT WHEN NOT HUNGRY

When you are not really hungry, food must be avoided. This is a most difficult thing to do, because the economics of life compel most of us to have regular meal times and we feel guilty if we do not eat food prepared for us. This is a definite point in favour of the uncooked diet, but unfortunately such a diet is not usually of value in the first stages of the cure of ulceration and therefore we have practically no choice but to take that of the cooked variety. So, therefore, perhaps the first thing you have to do in this case is to impress upon the person who is cooking that on some days you will be unable to take the food. This is often a rather disagreeable task, but can frequently be made less so by deciding long before the meal that you are not hungry.

If food is taken without desire, complications soon arise and digestion is impaired, with the result that indigestion and stomach heaviness rapidly follow. In the first stages of cure, especially, this is most undesirable because we are attempting to give the stomach and bowel time to heal and a fresh disturbance will only hamper matters and delay the cure. Many people will think on reading this that they would never eat at all because they are seldom conscious of the real hunger. That may be so, but when the whole course is in practice, hunger of the real variety will soon make its appearance.

At this stage, when the digestive tube is healing, it is common for the patient to experience a sudden great hunger which he or she cannot satisfy. This is a symptom which must be limited because this is a false hunger and means that the system is undergoing a healing change. Do not attempt to satisfy that hunger but rather keep to your normal diet and drink plenty of water.

DON'T OVEREAT

Once a meal is missed and natural hunger returns, care must be taken at the next meal not to overeat. Many do so in an effort to make up the amount of food previously missed. This often arises from the popular misconception that strength is generated in relation to the amount of food taken. The kind and amount of food assimilated and the efficiency of the eliminative apparatus have much more to do with this aspect of things.

When you avoid food for any time it is usual to find that the near relatives begin to get alarmed, and often uneasiness is conveyed to you. This is quite natural, for lack of appetite is wrongly but commonly assumed to be a bad sign. You must not, however, allow the thoughts of others to divert you from your purpose. Certainly under the circumstances you may feel tired and weak and although the negative suggestions of your friends may have something to do with this, it is mostly likely the result of reactions within your system. The body, recognizing the chance it is getting to heal will makes its own effort to cleanse the digestive tract and most impurities will come away. This is easily seen by the dirtiness of the tongue after missing a few meals, and you can understand that this cannot be corrected naturally by eating more food. Now, when this cleansing is taking place it is common to find that you become tired and headachy, due to the formation of gas in the bowel. The cure for this temporary condition lies in the taking of copious drinks of warm water.

NEVER EAT WHEN THE MOUTH IS DRY

When the body really desires food, the mouth becomes moist and this moisture increases at the sight, taste and smell of an appetizing meal. If the body does not desire food, no amount of enticement in the cooking and dressing of food will make the mouth water. Food must be avoided under all such circumstances. It is interesting to note the extreme dryness of the mouth in fevers and the treatment to which these patients are subjected in the dietetic sphere. So never take food when the mouth is dry, and keep the diet to liquid – mainly plain, fresh water. Do not take solids after this liquid on the assumption that the mouth is then moist. The moisture of the mouth should come from the glands within the mouth cavity, not from without, and as this action is under nervous and chemical control, it cannot be assisted by external means.

FOOD MUST BE THOROUGHLY CHEWED
Food should be semi-fluid before being swallowed and special attention must also be paid to the mastication of starchy foods, which include all flour products, cereals and rice. All starchy food must be chewed until it is sweet in the mouth before it is swallowed. This aids digestion, prepares the stomach, prevents over-eating and increases the assimilative powers of the stomach. Many people will have read of the danger of starchy foods in the formation of catarrh (often ulceration of the stomach originates in gastric catarrh) and much of this danger can be minimized by attention to prolonged chewing. The more you chew the less you need to eat, and the greater the benefit received.

FOOD SHOULD BE TAKEN DRY
In Nature Cure, milk is regarded as a solid food and therefore it does not interfere with the above rule. Dry food is slightly more difficult to digest than the solid and liquid mixtures, and it is this natural difficulty which retones the stomach and bowel internally because it means that the moisture of digestion is obtained from the salivary glands and not from external sources. Washing the food down weakens the digestive juices and so decreases assimilation of the minute food particles.

EAT ONLY NATURAL FOODS
If you grow your own vegetables and fruits, make sure that they are fed on natural fertilizers and are not unbalanced by artificial stimulation.

These are the actual food rules which are essential to good digestion, but they must be accompanied by a general rule which applies more to the emotional system than to any other. Digestion is a complicated business and has various controls from the mental, emotional, physical and chemical systems of the body. If one of these is below par, it shows signs which are easily recognized and which denote that the digestive system is not ready for food. For instance, if, after a hard day's work, a person feels very tired, there may be hunger, but the person feels that even to chew food is an effort. Food, therefore, should not be taken in this condition, because the muscular system of the stomach will also be tired and digestion will be impaired. If, however, a short rest is taken, say half an hour before the meal is served, the digestion will be satisfactory. The same applies when a person is emotionally upset after some continued worry, bout of anger, shock of an accident, anything of the nature which disturbs the emotional controls.

In all these conditions we are brought back to the rule of not eating when the mouth is dry, because this condition always occurs in emotional distress. This is again a difficult rule to follow, because it is against what has become the natural inclination. When you are distressed and your friends notice it, the first thing they do is to give a cup of tea or some stimulant to revive you. It is given in all kindness, but its after-effects may be deadly to the stomach, because food or liquid taken during great emotional distress becomes poisonous in the stomach within a very short time. If the stomach is comparatively healthy, the recipient is soon actively sick, a life-saving reaction, as it were. On the other hand, the person with the rather unhealthy stomach has not this immediate reaction and poisonous material is absorbed into the bowel. Eating and drinking at this time is one of the great primary causes of stomach ulceration. Statistics have shown that eating after a severe burn can lead directly to stomach ulceration; and the same applies to all forms of emotional upset, whether it be worry, anger, fear, or caused by accident or some dreadful shock.

SIX IMPORTANT RULES

Gathering all these vital rules together, we have six axioms which must be known by heart by all who suffer from digestive difficulty. If you keep to your diet strictly and have stomach pain, go over your axioms and you will certainly find that you have disobeyed at least one of them. On the other hand, if you obey these rules you can take some licence with your diet and not suffer from any discomfort. These rules are more important than any diet and I will enumerate them again:

1. Never eat when tired or emotionally upset.
2. Never eat when not hungry, even if it is meal time.
3. Never eat when the mouth is dry.
4. Masticate food thoroughly, especially the starchy food.
5. Eat only natural foods.
6. Take food as dry as possible.

4.
Breakfast

Once a soothing diet has been established with the aid of the diary, and the rules of eating and drinking thoroughly fixed in the mind, many sufferers will think that they are cured because the pain has been very much reduced. This is not the case, however; the stomach is only soothed and rested but not healed in any way and dietetic indiscretion will immediately set it going again. The real healing will take much longer than this – roughly one month for each year the trouble has been present, and it is proposed to start with the building of a diet which will ultimately, in conjunction with the other measures advocated in this book, bring about a complete and lasting cure.

FLUID ON RISING
The question whether to drink on wakening is one which raises great controversy in health circles and I can only given you the results of my experience. I have found that some people feel sick after taking the early morning drink and in these cases it is naturally inadvisable. Others feel their mouths dirty at this time, and in such cases either warm or cold water, to suit the taste, should be taken in quantity. Water, the universal solvent, is of great benefit in cleansing a dirty digestive tract, as shown by an unclean tongue. It must be

remembered that a dirty tongue and dryness of the mouth can arise from too little ventilation in the bedroom, and more fresh air will give good results.

You will read that the dry diet (without liquid) is the most beneficial of all, and certainly when it is indicated the results are often really wonderful. But it is only helpful in people who are carrying too much water in their systems due to underworking of the kidneys and skin. Water in such cases is only adding to the general confusion of the body, and may so weaken the bloodstream and reduce the tissue vitality that cure is impossible. These people thrive on the dry diet.

The spare person with more muscle than fat usually needs more liquid and, although this must be actually dictated by thirst, anything up to four pints daily is quite in order.

Summing up, therefore, on this question, it would appear sound that the person with flabby and watery tissues must only take fluid in small amounts and the thin person with the dehydrated tissues may take it in quantity. The condition of the tongue, however, should be the criterion of early morning fluid.

AVOID 'ACID' DRINKS
Most health books advise the taking of fresh acid juice first thing in the morning and while this is advantageous in many cases, it does not apply in gastric-duodenal troubles. The pouring of an acid straight to an inflamed stomach is wrong treatment and usually makes the condition very much worse. So, if you have acidity, avoid the acid fruit drinks such as lemon, apples, grapefruit, oranges and pineapple.

On the other hand, vegetable juices, extracted straight from the plant by a juice press, are strongly alkaline and may be used in small quantities at the beginning of the treatment and worked into larger amounts as progress is made. These juices are strongly alkaline, but may be too much so for the very sensitive stomach and small quantities such as a teaspoonful are enough to start with until it is decided whether they agree.

The dried-fruit juices, such as prunes, figs and raisins, are also alkaline in reaction, provided that plenty of water is taken with them, and may be given in larger amounts than the vegetable juices because they are generally more palatable.

Milk is too clogging for the early morning drink; and coffee or tea, which are poisons in minor degrees, wither and dry the stomach and make potential ulceration a reality. Avoid them completely.

Numerous patients tell me that they never have any trouble with their bowels but that they take a little salts every morning just to keep them right. This is a very pernicious habit which makes the bowel lazy, because it recognizes that means are being taken to introduce a mild poison which must be flung out if the body has to retain its integrity.

Soon that bowel will only work when it receives this poison and thus loses in its normal impetus. In addition to this, salt and other mild laxatives have an effect upon the tissues and other organs of elimination, especially the kidneys, and many people who suffer from obesity and nephritis never think that their trouble may be due to some salt laxative.

DO YOU NEED BREAKFAST?

The breakfast meal is usually a light one and, in many cases where the system is already overcrowded with impurities, this meal could with advantage be dispensed with altogether. If, however, the ulceration of the system is painful, it is not advisable to miss the breakfast meal; indeed, it is not advantageous ever to allow the stomach to be completely empty, because the inflamed edges of the wound come in contact with another part of the stomach and more pain results. So, in the first stages of treatment, the stomach should be kept in a state of continual digestion, or at least partly filled. This means that even although the desire for breakfast is not too great, some milk should be taken. Certain people will find that whole milk is too heavy, and half milk and half water should then be tried. If this is still too indigestible, the white of an egg should be switched up in about half a pint of water and this should be sipped at intervals during the morning.

STARCH AND FRUIT

If real hunger is present at the breakfast meal, the food should be given under two main headings, namely, starch and fruit. The starch can be provided by any bran or wholewheat breakfast cereal made from natural ingredients. Actually, such foods could be called the cleansing starches because they cleanse the bowel by introducing some mild roughage. However, it is advisable to 'ring the changes' with these cereals for a balanced diet.

Most people take milk with their cereals but this is not a good mixture and tends to create catarrh and acidity. It is much better to take cereals with the juice of dried fruit or, even better, to mix the cereal starch with the juice and whole of the fruit. It is important to note that dried fruits, namely prunes, figs and raisins, are acid in reaction if they are not thoroughly soaked overnight and then lightly stewed before serving.

The roughage cereal and the dried fruit form a very good combination, but if hunger is still present, more starch may be taken in the form of wholewheat bread, cut thin and toasted, then buttered cool. Many will find that digestive upset follows the taking of wholewheat toast and so, in these cases, white toast is allowed, buttered and toasted in the same manner. Crispbread and brown digestive biscuits are also allowable at this meal.

So far the breakfast meal outlined is finely arranged from

the dietetic viewpoint, and it is at this point that some difficulty arises because many people will feel that not enough food is allowed and will try to put in an egg or cheese. These are protein building foods which do not combine with the starches and should not be taken at this meal. If more food is desired it is better to keep to the starches – porridge or Slippery Elm food, for instance, both of these having beneficial effects on the digestive tube.

RAW SALADS

Vegetables also combine well with the dried fruit and starch, and raw grated carrot is now a favourite addition at the breakfast meal, and many also take a fresh raw salad. This may seem a very un-British breakfast, but even so it does not follow that the popular idea is the correct one. The taking of raw salad at this time, however, may cause some gastric disturbance and it is better to allow some weeks to pass before this form of food is introduced.

No milk or any other form of fluid should be taken at the breakfast meal, unless of course no solid food is desired. Milk, however, is allowed during the morning if the need for it is felt.

This primary change of diet should be gradual over a period of some two weeks and no other dietetic changes, except those found suitable by keeping a food diary, should be made.

5.
Water Treatment

Once the diet has been partly changed, the main effort must be directed towards retoning the general muscular system, especially the stomach area, because no lasting cure can be effected by dietetic treatment alone. Retoning means the alternate resting and invigorating of all the muscles and organs of the body and it can be fairly quickly brought about by the use of water and exercise.

In Nature Cure practice both warm and cold water applications are used, as also are certain medicated waters, but in the case of ulceration simple means are by far the most effective and the following regime will bring quick results. Again, however, I must stress that each individual varies with regard to water treatment and some must choose the cold and others the warm applications. It depends on the vitality of the patient and the reaction to cold water.

THE SOAPY SPONGE
With warm water and pure, natural soap, work up a good lather and apply plentifully to the stomach and bowel area. Keep rubbing this soapy lather into the skin for at least five minutes, then wash off with warm water. This treatment is best performed before retiring and may be followed by the cold compress with advantage. In certain cases, the warm

soapy lather may be covered with a flannel and allowed to dry on the part, but this should only be practised under professional advice.

Experience has shown that this is a most beneficial treatment in ulceration, although it is most difficult to prove anatomically or physiologically. It may be that it increases the drainage of the parts, or else that it invigorates the skin elimination. Whatever the reason, it does bring great relief in most cases. This treatment may be continued every night for two or three months and then should be discontinued for one month before recommencing.

THE COLD SPONGE

To people who like cold water and have a good brisk reaction, more benefit will be obtained from cold-water sponging (without soap) of the abdomen. This application should not last longer than two minutes and vigorous rubbing with a rough towel should follow. Once the fresh, warm blood is flowing through the stomach area and the part feels tightened and rejuvenated, give the chest and back a light, cold sponge and a brisk friction rubbing. This will prevent general chill and act as a bracing tonic, but care must be taken about the reaction: after such a treatment the patient must feel warm and invigorated. If, as often occurs, the reaction does not take place as usual, a warm drink such as yeast extract or soup should be taken to increase the vitality and prevent chilling.

THE FRICTION RUB

When the body will not react to the cold water, the skin circulation can be increase dby brisk friction, using the hands, a rough towel or friction gloves which are made for the purpose. In this treatment, take a small part of the body at a time and rub vigorously until the part becomes red and the blood appears very near the surface.

At the beginning of such treatment it is fairly easy to break the skin, but only a few mornings will elapse before the body can take a very vigorous rub without any harm. This treatment is most beneficial during the morning, and once the skin is working efficiently a little cold water should be rubbed into the skin with the hands until a quick, cold sponge is being taken. The friction and cold rubs are much more toning than the warm ones, and every effort should be made to gain an effective reaction.

THE COLD COMPRESS

Although the foregoing treatments (except the soapy sponge) have been mainly general in their action this does not mean that nothing is done to the abdomen itself. Nature Cure is a system of healing which believes in the wholeness of everything, but it also allows for local treatment – or at least an accentuation of the treatment on the main local condition. One such application is the cold compress, used very freely – often too freely – in the Nature Cure system. This application is primarily intended to increase the arterial blood circulation to the part and bring about the relief of congestion, but its technique must be thoroughly understood if a good result is to be obtained.

The best material to use as a compress is linen of good quality, but cotton can be used if linen is not obtainable. The thickness of the compress is also important, and it should be as thin as possible at the beginning of compressing because then it does not hold much water and is easily heated by the temperature of the body.

Stomach sufferers should cut a piece of linen of length such that it will just fit round the middle of the body and overlap one inch, for fixing with tapes or pins. The width of the linen should be about six inches and this may be gradually increased until the body is covered from under the breast to the hips. The compress, before applying, is dipped in cold water (or any kind of water advised) and wrung out thoroughly and then placed firmly round the waist. It should then be immediately covered with two or three layers of flannel or woollen material to initiate moist heat generation with the skin.

The patient should then retire to bed and, if the room is cold, hot water bottles may be placed on either side of the compress. Within ten minutes the compress should become warm. This is ascertained by placing the finger between the linen and the skin, when the heat will be felt. If this occurs, all is well, but if the compress feels cold and clammy it should be taken off, otherwise the body may become chilled.

It is impossible to determine the type of person who will respond to the compress, and it is always a case of trial and error at the beginning. If the compress does not heat, the body's vitality should be allowed to rise for another week or fortnight and the pack should be tried again and doubtless a good result will then be obtained. The compress may heat at the first application and continue to do so for weeks or even months, and then suddenly the reaction is lost and the compress will not become warm in spite of all effort. This need cause no alarm because it often happens, and it usually means that the healing vitality of the body is being directed elsewhere. Stop compressing for a week and then try again.

As I have said, the compress is usually applied at night and kept on during all the sleeping hours. Many people will think that this is uncomfortable, but the opposite is the case and it is often difficult to get a patient to desist from compresses because he finds the application most soothing and sleep-giving. In all such cases the body is using the skin as an outlet and is in dire need of relief.

WHEN NOT TO APPLY A COMPRESS

Never apply a compress when the body is exhausted. The reaction is always below normal in such cases and there is a danger of chilling.

Never apply a compress immediately before or during the menstrual period.

Never apply a local compress without having one on the waist at the same time.

LOCAL COMPRESSES

A local compress means the application of wet linen to a part other than the waist, and in stomach cases it is usually applied to the neck to relieve nervous tension of the area and allow a sufficient nerve flow from the brain to the stomach. The neck compress is applied exactly as for the waist, except that a narrow strip of linen, about three inches wide, is used. In nearly every case this compress will heat quickly. The neck compress should never be applied without one on the waist, unless on professional advice, because there is a tendency to draw impurities to the part, and more harm may result. This is counteracted by the large abdominal compress.

Immediately the diet has been changed, compressing can be commenced, starting with the waist, and, provided the reaction is good, this method of treatment may be continued for a month or two on five nights per week.

6.
The Second Meal

Once the starchy/dried-fruit breakfast has been instituted for two to three weeks, a gradual change can be worked on the second meal. Usually the best one to change is the midday one which, because of the tendency to have protein (body-building) foods included, is the one most likely to cause certain forms of acidity. Another point is that the midday meal is often rushed and too much food is taken in too limited a space of time. This leads, as explained in the rules of eating, to fermentation and pain in the stomach.

Commonly, soup is the first thing taken at this meal, and all sufferers from indigestion look upon this liquid with a cautious eye. Actually some form of soup can be taken with ease by most people, but I think it advisable in all cases of ulceration to avoid soup completely, at least for the first six months of dieting.

The protein part of the meal, consisting of meat, fish, fowl, cheese, egg, nuts, peas, beans and lentils, is acid forming. Small quantities of these foods are allowed, but their reaction must always be carefully studied. Red meat is best and should be grilled or casseroled. White meat is very acid forming, although easy of digestion, and it is not advised under any circumstances. Fish is allowed once or twice weekly, but it is a

THE SECOND MEAL 35

negative food and it must be steamed and never taken more frequently.

Cheese puddings may be used frequently if they suit the particular digestion. Eggs should be lightly boiled, poached or scrambled, but never fried. Peas, beans and lentils are ideal forms of protein but are inclined to clog the bowel when taken in too great amounts.

PROTEIN DISTRIBUTION

Here is a list of the way in which the proteins should be distributed:

Sunday – Meat or egg
Monday – Cheese
Tuesday – Egg
Wednesday – Peas and beans
Thursday – Fish
Friday – Meat or egg
Saturday – Cheese.

Variations of this can be made to suit individual taste, but only one protein should be taken at one meal and one protein per day is sufficient for any adult. Overeating of proteins leads to acidity, and blood and heart diseases.

With the protein part of the meal it is necessary to take some form of vegetable to neutralize the acidity. Cabbage, carrot, turnip, beetroot, cauliflower, parsnip, etc., are ideal. These vegetables should be steamed or cooked in the casserole to retain the valuable mineral salts. Boiled vegetables are useless.

The amount of vegetable taken at the midday meal need not be large, and three or four tablespoonsful will be sufficient for sensitive stomachs at the beginning of the treatment. However, every effort must be made to increase this quantity as the stomach hardens up. Sometimes it will be necessary to stop the vegetables and have recourse to the milk diet, but whenever the stomach becomes quiet again, the vegetables must be reintroduced.

Once it is possible to take whole meals of vegetables, either raw or steamed, the digestive trouble is well on the way to recovery. Steamed and baked vegetables are alkaline in reaction, but they are not so beneficial as the raw ones and these will be introduced in greater quantities in the later stages of the cure.

POTATOES

It will be noted that potatoes are not mentioned as good mixtures with the proteins. This is because they are mainly formed of starch, good starch, beneficial to acid sufferers, but not suitable when mixed with proteins because of the tendency to create a false appetite. Potatoes, steamed or baked (never boiled), should be taken at the evening meal, which will be discussed later.

DESSERT

The dessert always presents a difficulty in the protein meal, and experience proves that it is best avoided. The dried fruits, however, because of their alkalinity, combine very well with the proteins and may be taken. Once the stomach trouble has lost its acuteness, the acid fruits may also be given raw or lightly cooked. Often these fruits agree when no starch is taken at the same meal, but it would appear much wiser to leave them out of the diet until the first three months have passed. There are exceptions to this rule, however, in certain forms of dyspepsia in which the acid content is low and then there is an actual craving for acid fruits. This should be satisfied.

Instead of the fruit dessert it is often advisable to give a glass of milk. This is actually breaking the rule of taking only one protein at a meal, because milk is a protein, but it is frequently very soothing to a very irritated stomach and is not so harmful in most cases as the combination of other proteins such as cheese and egg or meat and cheese. The practice of taking steamed and milk puddings after the midday meal is not permissible because it again breaks the rule of not mixing starches and proteins. The puddings should be taken with the later meal, which will be a starchy one.

In a nutshell, then, we have the midday or second meal as follows:

Proteins – Meat, fish, eggs, cheese, milk, peas, beans and lentils (one of the above only)

with

Vegetables – All kinds of steamed and baked vegetables except potatoes

Fruit – Dried or fresh acid fruit.

No condiments, sauces or preserves should be used with the above meals, and no water or any kind of fluid should be taken at the meal. Needless to say, small quantities and prolonged mastication are also essential. If you are thirsty it is advisable to take water before the meal, because if taken afterwards there is a tendency to 'bag' the stomach, causing it to fall and place more strain on the irritated area.

People who have been in the habit of taking an alkaline medicine with such a meal should not stop this treatment drastically, but should reduce the quantity slowly each week until it is felt that it is no longer necessary.

Ulcerations of the digestive system are greatly irritated by cold weather, and care must be taken to prevent the body – especially the feet – from getting chilled. The same applies to the taking of very hot and very cold foods and drinks. Extremes should always be avoided. Many a cure is completely upset by the taking of ice-cream or iced water.

7.
Exercising the Abdomen

Strictly speaking, the most suitable internal stomach exercise is brought about by the dietetic changes, because the power of the stomach musculature will increase due to the need for more effort in dealing with foods which are difficult to digest. In the same way as an arm is never made strong by keeping it in a sling, the stomach thrives on natural foods which make it work more efficiently if the body is to receive full benefit.

This is the great mistake of the ordinary medical methods of treating stomach and bowel ulceration. The weakness of the stomach is accepted, and the organ is fed on foods which are always easy to digest. The result is that such a stomach will not attempt to digest the more difficult foods and so it must be retrained. This training is brought about internally by the type of food and externally by simple exercises which retone the muscles of the abdomen and, after some time, the muscles of the stomach and bowel.

Abdominal exercises should be practised systematically morning and night, but the muscles must never be overstrained. When it is felt that certain muscles cannot perform an exercise it should be discontinued until more physical strength is attained. This is why we advise only a limited number of movements at first with the provision that the movements must be practised as regularly as possible.

THE FIRST EXERCISE

Purpose – For raising the abdomen and lifting any prolapsed organs back to their original places. Ideal for constipation.

Position – Lie on the back, completely relaxed with the knees bent and the feet on the floor. Slowly pull the abdomen inwards and towards the head. Hold for a few seconds and then relax. Perform this primary exercise about ten times, gradually increasing as the muscles grow stronger.

THE SECOND EXERCISE

Purpose – For strengthening the ligaments and muscles which hold the abdomen and bowels in the erect position.

Position – Standing erect with the hands clasped behind the back, slowly draw the abdomen inwards until it is felt that the entire abdomen, and especially the lower part just above the pubic bones, has been lifted upwards and inwards. This exercise, to be performed properly, requires very good muscular tone and usually some difficulty is experienced at the beginning. However, perseverance will soon bring about a great improvement. The abdomen should be held up as long as possible without overtiring. It is common to find that the muscles are sore after this exercise has been performed for the first few times.

Start with these two exercises and continue with them for two or three weeks, night and morning, gradually increasing the number of movements. If by this time you feel that the muscles have increased in power and tone, you can start the third and fourth movements, but if the muscles have not improved very much you should continue with the first two movements for at least another fortnight.

THE THIRD EXERCISE

Purpose – To exercise the liver, kidneys, pancreas and spleen.

Position – Stand erect with the hands on the waist. Bend

slowly to the side as far as possible without overstraining, keeping the body erect and the abdomen in and up. Try to feel some compression of the internal organs between the ribs and the top of the hip bone. Now bend to the other side, also trying to get this feeling of pressure. The exercise becomes much more beneficial if deep breathing is practised at the same time. Breathe in as you bend to the right and out when going to the left side. Continue in this sequence for a number of movements and then change the breathing, drawing the breath in as you bend to the left and exhaling as you go to the right. Start with twelve movements to each side.

THE FOURTH EXERCISE
Purpose – To re-tone the external abdominal muscles.

Position – Lying on the back, lift one leg to right angles, lower and then raise the other. Do not allow the legs to touch the floor or table after lowering. This is a much more strenuous exercise, and care must be taken at first because it is very easy to strain the muscles. It is an exercise which is easy to perform if the person is used to long walks and therefore, if it is very difficult at first, fairly long walks should be taken with the deliberate intention of strengthening the muscles.

Once these four exercises can be practised with ease and without any physical strain, the fifth and last exercise should be started. This is difficult mainly because of the position assumed before commencing the movement, but practice will bring its reward.

THE FIFTH EXERCISE
Purpose – To allow the abdominal contents to fall into their original positions.

Position – Lie on back with pillow (high) under hips and the hips supported as high as possible with the hands. In this position perform cycling movements with the legs, making these movements as large and full as possible. As I have said, the original position is the most difficult to acquire because the hips should be kept at *right angles* to the body. Once, however, this position is reached and the balance kept, the rest of the exercise is easy.

These five exercises should be practised for ten minutes, night and morning, after the muscles have become accustomed to the new movements. By themselves they are not sufficient to rebuild the stomach and increase the nerve supply and blood drainage of the parts, but when combined with water treatments, especially compressing, and a balanced diet, their effect is very marked.

The abdominal lift should be practised at all times, whether walking, sitting or lying, and soon the tension on the muscles will become so natural that it will be done unconsciously.

8.
The Third Meal

Formerly, dietitians of the Nature Cure School were inclined to place great stress on the intake of fresh acid fruit, but years of experience have proved that this class of food is not of benefit in special groups of symptoms, and ulcerations of the digestive tract come within this category. On the other hand, the value of mixed raw vegetables in these conditions has been proved completely and therefore the third meal of your diet should be a starchy vegetable one.

These vegetables must be taken raw in the form of a salad, and this may lead to some slight digestive upset because the abnormally sensitive stomach will be irritated by the hard edges of these cleansers and vitalizers. Patience and perseverance, however, will bring rewards which will recompense you many times over for this initial discomfort. The complete digestion of the vegetables with rigid control of the emotions and the following of the dictates of natural appetite are the secrets of the cure.

Start the introduction of the vegetables by giving a small amount of grated carrot. If this agrees, give some grated turnip and then lettuce, watercress, mustard and cress. Onions and grated cabbage are more difficult to digest and will upset many a normal stomach. Treat them with respect. The tomato, greatest fruit addition to the salad, is also inclined to be acid and must be taken in very small quantities at the beginning. It may be said about the tomato that a great deal depends upon where it has been grown and whether compost and natural manures have been used. Grown naturally it will be found palatable to even the most sensitive stomach.

CHOOSE ORGANICALLY GROWN FOOD

Although I have mentioned tomatoes specifically in this connection, the same applies to the growing of every vegetable, and where possible no artificial manures should be used and forced vegetable and fruit growing stopped. Vegetables and fruits are the health regulators of our bodies and pour their medicines and correctives straight from the soil into our bodies. It follows then that we must make every effort to keep our soil in a clean and healthy condition, and to grow the plants with the minimum of artificiality.

The vegetables should be the main part of the third meal when experience has proved that the stomach and bowel juices can deal with them. This will naturally take time and training, which cannot be rushed, so small amounts of vegetables must be the rule at the beginning. It may be that this amount will only be enough for the filling of wholewheat sandwiches using lettuce, carrot, turnip, celery, tomato and watercress. Afterwards it is better if the vegetables are taken apart from the starch, a separation which allows more prolonged chewing.

The meals in which the raw vegetables are taken should never be hurried, and time is most advantageous to the stomach sufferer. The mineral salts and vitamins which are supplied by fresh raw vegetables can only be obtained by a thorough breaking up of all particles of the plants and in doing so a stomach reaction which will make the assimilation of these vital foods comparatively easy is ensured.

THE VALUE OF SALADS
The frame of mind in which the salad meal is approached is
most important. It must not be regarded as a necessary evil,
but rather as a natural and health-giving procedure which will
release health-giving material into the body. Many people
will pass sarcastic remarks about your salad eating and refer to
your 'rabbit food'. These remarks, however, need not hinder
your efforts to find out the desires of your body. The mind
must be kept open to the suggestions of the mind and body,
and not swayed by external influences of others. Carry on
with the experiment of finding how your health can be
regenerated by food and thought, and do not allow the
uninitiated to place a trace of doubt within your mind.

We are only now beginning to see the light with regard to
diet and the balancing of food, and you can do much by
recording your experience of these findings. Nature Cure is
very thoroughly based upon proved facts, but its later findings
depend on the exploration of avenues which are opening daily
from these bases. The practitioners of this method of living
have certainly the best chance of increasing this knowledge
but suffer in the respect that the demands upon their services
become so great that prolonged and deep study is most
difficult.

The rest of the meal should be composed of starchy foods.
These include potatoes, whole rice products, whole grains of
all kinds such as bread, scone, biscuits, fruit-cakes. You will
have read of the dangers of starchy food and of its causative
tendencies in all forms of acidity. Many of these statements are
true but there is a tendency to overrate the negative aspects of
starchy food.

Starch is a necessity in our lives to give heat and energy and
it must be taken. In practice I find that many patients are
actually suffering from a lack of starch rather than too much.
The amount of starch taken by a person on the ordinary diet is

no real guide to the amount taken into (assimilated by) the body, although it may show the amount of bowel activity. When these people start on a Nature Cure diet and reduce their starch considerably and quickly the end result is often that they show signs of general weakness, especially lack of energy.

HOW MUCH STARCH?

I cannot give you rules with regard to amounts in ounces of the starch required by each individual, because that is impossible, but I believe that if you are following all the guidelines set down in this book, the body will regulate its starch intake itself and when you are taking too much starch or sugar it will give its warnings by the appearance of some skin eruptions or by some form of catarrhal discharge.

This latter method of elimination may occur from the ear, from the throat and chest and nose, from the bowel in the form of colitis, or from the womb as leucorrhoea. It is a warning rather than a definite disease and when appreciated by the sufferer in this light it can be treated by starch reduction and correct food combination. Reading this you may think that this is always an easy thing to cure. In fact it is not in many cases, because with a reduction in the foods which are causing the trouble you may get some cessation of the eruption or discharge and then the body, recognizing your effort to help it, may use this channel to clear itself of many more impurities. This means, of course, that the discharge will get worse and may last for weeks and even months before it stops.

When this state of affairs is reached, it is the most difficult thing in the world to keep the patients from trying all sorts of suppressive measures, such as douches and ointments, and yet the use of these leads to far greater trouble, because the body, stopped in its cleansing efforts, seems to lose faith, and the trouble turns inwards to reappear in a few years in a much more virulent if not malignant form. Suppression of discharge is the one thing which must not be done. It is the straight path to ill-health, but it is undoubtedly difficult to resist trying anything if a discharge is uncomfortable.

9.
The Progress of the Cure

Many stomach sufferers on reading this book will decide to choose certain parts of the advice and apply them to their particular case. Such a course will never be successful, for this is a *whole* treatment, based on bringing the entire body into line, so allowing the healing vitality which lies within the body to work. Any taking out of parts of the scheme will be followed by failure, and may cause other organs of the body to work faultily.

The purpose behind the giving of the various dietetic changes at rather prolonged intervals is twofold. Firstly, it is intended to prevent the inflamed and irritated parts of the stomach and bowel from becoming more sensitive on the passage of natural foods, which have rather hard exteriors, and which need efficient digestion.

Secondly, it is arranged in this manner to prevent too rapid a change from below-par health to cleansing health, because the latter state results in a throwing-out of impurity. It will stop this cleansing from becoming too vigorous. Slow change is followed by gradual increase in health without a great deal of upset and is always advisable in adult life. If, however, a vigorous cleansing is wanted in a young patient, the amount of fresh acid fruit should be increased, and quicker healing will result due to the positive salts contained in these lively foods.

AFTER AN OPERATION

If a surgical operation has been undergone previous to this treatment, it does not mean that a complete cure by the suggested methods is impossible, but rather that the cure will be prolonged. It will also ensure that the complication of gastric and duodenal ulcer operations, namely appendicitis, will be prevented by the general cleansing and retoning of the bowel.

Scar tissue adhesions present the worst features of these operations and the use of the cold abdominal compress continuously over a long period is imperative in the curing and prevention of this condition. In such cases, when the stomach and bowel have reached the stage in which fasting on water only does not cause any discomfort, one day per week without food will also be of great benefit in removing adhesions.

It should be noted that if the abdominal pain ever becomes severe, recourse to milk and Slippery Elm food should be immediate. This is actually giving the digestive organs a partial rest, thus allowing healing to proceed and, at the same time, it prevents the excess acid in the digestive tract doing harm. If such an upset cannot be traced to some dietetic or emotional indiscretion and you have been feeling particularly well before it occurred, it may be assumed that it is a healing crisis and that nothing but benefit will follow the treatment suggested.

The theoretical treatment would be immediate fasting, with cold compresses, and only water to drink, but in practice it is usually better to take milk and a small amount of bland food. No medicines, not even laxatives, should be taken. Once the stomach has readjusted itself, it will be found that it is more powerful and that difficult foods can be digested with ease. If you decide to use alkaline medicines you will entirely destroy all the benefit which has been obtained.

PROMPT RESPONSE

Soon after starting the treatment, you will notice that the pain and discomfort is not so severe as previously. This is due to the more positive dietary which feeds all the tissues of the body, quietens the nerves and increases the power of impurity elimination by giving the organs which perform this function less work to do.

Actually your body begins to work more efficiently at a lower rate, and your pulse will slow and the blood pressure drop. This means more rest for the heart, less strain on the arteries and a reduction in general wear and tear.

The water treatment for the skin is also designed to increase elimination. It may seem peculiar that skin attention will help in the cure of a stomach complaint: in actual professional Nature Cure practice, however, the skin is frequently the first tissue treated before any attention is paid to the painful area. In every disease benefit will follow skin care, especially of the part of the body over the painful area. Wash, scrub, rub and exercise the outer covering until it perspires and you will greatly aid the throwing out of impurities which are keeping you in ill-health.

The methods outlined here are mainly for people who cannot attend a trained Nature Cure practitioner for personal treatment. Naturally this would be the best way of treating any trouble, and skilled manipulation and osteopathic massage will often cure when all other means have failed.

THE SPINAL NERVES

It is common to find in such cases that one of the spinal nerves leading to the digestive tract has become caught in such a way that the nerve flow to the organ is impaired. This is easily discovered by a practitioner trained in the art of palpating these lesions and a few manipulative treatments will bring rapid relief. Frequently the practitioner also finds that although the spinal nerves are not impinged, they are irritated by rheumatic deposits high in the neck, a condition which often accompanies stomach ulceration and when these deposits are removed by massage and heat treatment gastric relief is immediately evident.

'LOOSE' ACIDITY

During the progress of cure, a certain amount of acidity will be loose in the system and slight twinges of rheumatism may be felt in the various joints, especially in the spine between and around the shoulder blades. These are but passing symptoms and the accumulations will be washed away to the kidneys and the skin glands for elimination. If uncomfortable, however, the pain can be eased by the application of alternate hot and cold packs and massage treatment. Under no circumstances should any sedatives or ointments be used because of their tendency to again suppress that which you have been striving to eliminate.

Strict adherence to the points outlined during the first few weeks of treatment will be sufficiently habit-forming to prevent the treatment from becoming an obsession and under no circumstances should the condition of your digestive system be allowed to control your life. Remember that in good health you are not aware that you have a stomach and this is the ideal at which you must aim.

With this in mind study where you have gone wrong, outline a course of treatment based upon the above lines and keep to it, allowing the inherent vitality within your body to do its work without hindrance. Do not worry about the length of treatment but remember that it has taken a long time for you to become ill, that a shorter period is needed for full recovery by the above methods and that a condition of health is being made available to you which will again make life a worthwhile experience.

10.
Ensuring a Healthy Start

Through following the simple rules of sensible eating, the sufferer will not only obtain great benefits with regard to the affected organs but will also find that generally the whole body will benefit. I have stressed before that you cannot single out one part of the body and treat it alone so, therefore, great benefit will result throughout the complete body system. Many sufferers have also felt a great change mentally as well as physically – after years of just living, and that must include unhealthy living, it is possible to find a new enthusiasm for life.

With all the pressures of twentieth-century life and habits, together with a continual bombardment of advertising, many people actually think it is natural to begin the day with some form of salts or medication and to end the day by falling asleep under the effects of a sleeping pill. In between, one takes pills after meals, for headaches and for lack of energy. The drug companies have never had it so good. However, this is not real living, as any thinking individual realizes.

THE IMPORTANCE OF DIET
Under Nature Cure principles, and these after all are just rules of plain sensible living, people realize that the human body can only take so much. In many households more attention is

paid to the diet of the family pet, with special care taken to make sure that its fur has a fine glossy sheen, than to the health and wellbeing of the family. It is up to responsible parents to look after and educate their children in healthy living, and so here I will devote a section to the prevention of the troubles that the reader may well wish had been instilled into him at an early age.

Many parents may find that, with their own diet amendments to help gastric troubles, the whole family can participate and general household diet changes can take place to the benefit of all.

As in all things there are exceptions to the rule. A few people eat to excess and never seem to suffer, or smoke heavily with apparently no ill effects. But you can be sure that these people are rare, and the gamble they take does not always pay off. Medical science has left us in no doubt of the validity of what Nature Cure principles have long advocated, and a healthy diet in many cases is prescribed by some individual general practitioners. However, health comes with healthy living, so it is best to start the young on the road to healthy adulthood.

WEANING

Formerly it was the practice to wean the child from breast milk to solid food in a short period, and in consequence the parents suffered many sleepless and worrying nights. Nowadays it is appreciated that gradual weaning over a period varying from three to four weeks is a much more sensible way of changing the dietary, and is one which benefits both the child and the mother, to say nothing of the peace of mind of the father.

In weaning, the first solid meal introduced should be a fruit one. Sieved prunes, figs, grated or stewed apples or pears or dates (mashed and cooked as a porridge with a little milk) are ideal for the purpose. Usually no great difficulty will be encountered with this meal because the digestive system of the child is already used to fruit juices. Vary the fruit from day to day, with as much variety as possible, and continue with the fruit meal for a week before making another change. Breast milk feeding should be continued at the other meals but the amount of liquid taken by the mother should be slightly reduced. If the breast is painfully full at breakfast time, the milk should be released by a breast pump.

The next meal, changed during the second week of weaning, should be limited to steamed vegetables and steamed or baked potatoes. Again as many varieties of vegetable as possible should be used, and the addition of a little butter will make the meal more palatable. However, no form of meat gravy is advised since the strain which meat imparts upon the liver and kidney may cause harm at this stage. A small amount of cow's milk may be given with the meal. During the second week the mother should again reduce the amount of liquid she is taking, and this combined with the lack of nipple stimulation will gradually result in reduced milk secretion in a normal fashion.

The third meal, changed during the third week, should consist of a small amount of vegetable soup, made without meat, and some starch in the form of wholewheat toast or rusk or whole rice pudding. Honey in small portions is also allowed, with milk if the child desires more liquid, although this is not an ideal addition because of the starch in the meal. The mother's diet must be kept low in liquid and whenever weaning has been accomplished the breast should be frequently sponged with cold water to ensure thorough drainage. Breast and abdominal exercises should be started to regain muscular control of these parts.

FOODS TO AVOID

The child must be trained from the very start of solid feeding to take and appreciate the foods which are health-giving and disease-resisting, and must be kept away from all other foods. At this stage there is one common dietetic error which must be guarded against, and that is the giving of milk with any form of starch. Such a mixture results in a gluey paste and is a frequent forerunner of catarrh. This means that the following mixtures are *not* advised:

1. Bread or biscuit with milk. (Bread with vegetables is a better mixture.)

2. Milk puddings. (These should never be given.)

3. Porridge with milk. (Take with prune juice, or better still as date porridge.)

Note: Milk should be given with the fruit and vegetable meals. It should never be boiled.

Such a scheme of weaning does not usually result in any insurmountable difficulties and it ensures that the child 'starts right' with solid food. The food given at this time is most important, and has a great bearing on future health as little dietetic errors at the weaning stage may result in grave bodily defects in later life.

The child is more digestively comfortable and therefore less fretful during prolonged weaning, since what has become his normal food is not completely and suddenly stopped. Solid food need digestive readjustment. This is often a slow process requiring patience and the gradual introduction of little changes in the diet, for this is a period when certain parts of the bowel and liver are being used for the first time. It also means that the liver is being provided with food which gives rise to great power and energy. If the correct foods are established this organ will get acquainted with them and will in future reject foods which are injurious. This training of intelligent choice on the part of the liver is one of the most valuable parts of natural dietetic living.

MOTHER SHARES THE BENEFIT

The mother also shares in the benefit of regulated weaning since the call upon her milk is not suddenly stopped, as was the usual custom some years ago. Under such conditions the tendency was to be left with full breasts and tight lacing and the taking of salt to reduce the milk was the common practice. These measures in certain ca~'s were successful and without harm, but in some women the complication of choked breast ducts arose. This usually resulted in inflammation of the breast (mastitis), a condition which, when treated by suppressive measures, has the tendency to recur in later life as a breast tumour.

With quick weaning it is also common to find that nervous women with poor circulation are inclined to become suddenly thin and suffer from emotional upsets, so that patience and regulation of diet are required to bring them back to normal health. This condition may occur also in prolonged weaning, but it is never so upsetting to the mother.

Breast feeding should be continued for nine months or even longer, and there is actually no cause for alarm if the child refuses to be weaned to a more solid diet until the age of one year. This is because, generally speaking, the milk of the mother is much to be preferred to the more solid food which has become customary in our age.

TEETHING

Many parents view the early arrival of teeth with pride, but in fact it is usually a warning of weakness in the mother's milk which results in the need for the means of chewing solid food. If this happens, breast feeding should be continued with positive changes in the mother's diet and the feeding of small amounts of solid food to the baby. In such cases, the breast feeding may still last the full nine months if the nipples do not become painful and inflamed. If this latter condition does arise weaning should be started immediately.

On the other hand, the late arrival of teeth is also not too good a sign. It usually denotes some lack of mineral salt, particularly calcium, in the milk and the mother's diet may require a much larger proportion of vegetables and milk. This is one of the reasons why I advocate the taking of milk during pregnancy. It does much to keep ·· the supply of calcium salts and it is given in a form which is in common usage and is not strange to the bowel.

Many mothers, going on a diet for the first time, are starved of mineral salts because they are being supplied with their vegetables in a different form — raw or steamed instead of boiled. This means that the bowel must act more efficiently to extract the valuable salts. Indeed, certain people do not extract these salts until a month or two has passed. This must be taken into account by the newcomer to diet reform, and usually a certain amount of overfeeding at first is permissible. The taking of milk does much to prevent mineral deficiency in such cases, although it may cause more bowel sluggishness.

PHYSICAL 'MAKE-UP'

The physical 'make-up' of the child is a vital factor during the stage of teething, and it is practically impossible to determine beforehand whether a child will have difficulty in cutting teeth. Many children pass through this stage with no greater upset than a slight restlessness, while others experience considerable pain and general distress. In the latter case, the appetite is lost and the child loses weight and the muscles become flabby.

If the lips and mouth feel hot and the child is putting his fingers on the gum and there is copious salivation, there is no need to worry. The treatment resolves itself into sympathetic nursing and the withholding of food until the child shows a readiness to eat. The dryness-of-the-mouth warning is present, and the lost weight will soon be regained. But if the child is fed when the lips are hot and the mouth tender, some harm may be done and it is likely that vomiting will follow the giving of food. This may ultimately result in indigestion and flatulence. The use of teething powders or any other forms of medication will only by followed by stomach upset. I have never had a case treated in this fashion which showed any beneficial result.

Many doctors advise small amounts of aspirin to very young infants passing through the teething stage. It is most doubtful if this relieves the pain. Certainly it brings about stomach and kidney upset. The use of medicine at this very early stage invariably assures later trouble. Treat by fasting and cold water, allowing the bowel to function naturally without castor oil or patent so-called syrups.

MILD FEVERS
Severe teething upsets often reach the stage of mild fevers with a certain amount of chest catarrh (called teething bronchitis). Sometimes an examination by a practitioner is necessary to determine that no other complications are present. This condition is much more common in bottle-fed babies and those who have been reared on dried milk. It should be treated by fasting on water only, or by small amounts of acid fruit juice.

If the condition is prolonged, the child appears to be failing and there is a danger of the mother communicating her alarm, then white of egg water (white of egg switched up in one pint of cold water) may be given freely. This will be found most soothing to the mouth and will also help to build the body. It will usually be found in such cases that the roof of the palate is high: this means that bulky starchy foods much be reduced and the child fed on fruit, vegetables and milk.

To enable the teeth to pierce the gums, hard substances must be given to chew. Bone rings and dried bones are the most suitable because these are usually flat and accomplish their object of clearing away the gum without filling the entire mouth cavity. This latter state is often brought about by the giving of rusks and pieces of hard toast in too great amounts. The mouth is filled with too much material and the palate is forced upwards, with the result that the mouth cavity becomes high and arched. This may be the sign of a good singer, but in the very young it is a condition which is often followed by much physical discomfort. The high palate compresses the nasal passage and tends to make the child a mouth breather and a sufferer from adenoids. So, when helping the teeth through the gum, remember that the palate must not be disturbed by the objects given to the child.

Usually I find that manufactured rusks are too large and are not hard enough, and that thin but hard pieces of wholewheat toast are better in every way. Care must be taken at this stage that an infant does not receive a fright when the toast or rusk is in the mouth. It is easy for the food to get stuck at the back of the throat and often great difficulty is experienced in clearing since the infant has not the muscular expulsive power of the older child or adult.

11.
Food in Childhood

From nine months to one year the child will progress very satisfactorily on a dietetic regime similar to that advocated during weaning, except that the amounts will gradually require increasing as the child gains in weight. Until the age of eighteen months has been reached the diet should be mainly milk, vegetables and fruit with little additions of starchy foods and occasionally, after one year has been reached, an egg once per week to add variety.

Building foods are essential at this time, but if limited to milk and eggs they are supplied in a form which does not throw great strain on the cleansing system. This is very important. It has been the experience of most practitioners that many forms of ill health owe their origin to overworking of the organs of elimination at this early stage, and if these organs are nursed and protected in infancy the expectancy of a healthy adult life is very much increased. The kidneys are usually the first organs to show the strain of wrong protein feeding. They are adversely affected by flesh foods and also by liquids such as tea, coffee and aerated waters, and it is a parent's duty to the child to keep these foods out of his diet during the first few years.

SUGGESTED DIET UP TO EIGHTEEN MONTHS
Breakfast   Milk and fruit or fruit and fruit juices.

Lunch   Small amount of vegetable soup;
           Steamed vegetables;
           Glass of milk.
or   Lightly cooked egg occasionally;
           Steamed vegetables;
           Dried fruit.
or   Glass of milk;
           Steamed vegetables;
           Dried fruit.
Tea   Soup (only if actually desired);
           Wholewheat bread, butter, honey;
           Dried fruit such as prunes or figs.
or   Milk (if there is actual thirst);
           Baked potato with butter;
           Wholewheat biscuit, dates, bananas.
or   Baked potatoes;
           Steamed vegetables;
           Toasted wholewheat bread or scone;
           Dried fruit.

Fruit and vegetable juices may be given freely between meals.

There are several points which are interesting to note in this diet. Firstly, all white flour products including milk puddings are not advised and white sugar (a stomach irritant) does not receive mention. Meat and fish are not advantageous and conditments, preserves, and liquids like tea and coffee must be avoided.

The breakfast meal of fruit and milk is a completely balanced health-giving one which would be wasted by the addition of any form of starch. It will also be noted that in one alternative lunch meal, potatoes and milk are combined. In this case the starch is a natural one and does not give rise to a paste-like mixture. In all other meals where starch and milk are combined, the milk is given before the starch.

In every case the amount of soup should be limited. I find

that excessive soup intake weakens the digestive juices and tends to make the child flabby; and if meat stock is used, this fluid becomes a problem first to the digestive apparatus, and then to the kidneys. Kidney weakness and excessive laxness of the tissues go hand in hand, and the proteins are the foods which must be studied when this condition becomes apparent. Firmness of the muscles and tissues should be the ideal in every child no matter what the build, because it is a sign of good tone and means that internally the child is also in good health, for tone of the muscles and skin mirror the internal condition at every age.

With growth the child expends more and more energy and an increase in starchy food is required, although great care must be exercised that such food is not given in excessive quantities. In cases where the mastication is not thorough this should be corrected before more energy foods are added.

SUGGESTED DIET UP TO THREE YEARS

Breakfast   Fresh acid fruit such as apple or orange with small helping of dried fruit added. In the winter time more dried fruit than acid fruit should be taken. One glass of cold milk.

Lunch   Vegetable, tomato or lentil soup; Steamed vegetable with two baked potatoes; Small amount of wholewheat pudding or whole rice pudding. Fruit may be taken for dessert if the pudding is not desired.

Tea   Wholewheat toast or scone with dates, figs or honey. Crispbread or wholewheat biscuit may be given in place of this toast. Glass of milk, slightly warmed if desired.

Fresh fruit may be given between meals, or raisins if the weather is cold.

The child should be taught to chew all foods very

thoroughly and no liquid should be given to wash solid foods over the stomach. The practice of dipping biscuit and bread in milk is most harmful and is one certain way of creating stomach ill health. Prolonged chewing means that the stomach is thoroughly prepared for the food which is coming down and in real hunger the juices are often flowing before the food gets to the stomach. Chewing of starchy foods is especially valuable because the digestion of starch should take place primarily in the mouth and such food should taste sweet before being swallowed. Careful chewing of starch also means that less is taken and more benefit is obtained; this is very important because starch poisoning is the most common cause of illness in modern life.

BEWARE OF WHITE SUGAR
Manufactured and refined sugar are common stomach irritants in young children (and for that matter in adults), therefore all cakes, sweets and jams must be carefully regulated if health is to be maintained or regained. No food should be sweetened with sugar. If for any reason sweetening is required, honey and Barbardos sugar are the only allowable agents. Dried fruits, including prunes, figs, dates and raisins, are the ideal sources of natural sugar and the acid fruits also contain small amounts. The child should be taught that these fruits are the natural sugars and that all refined sugars are harmful in the extreme.

Starchy food is required during childhood to supply energy and it is an essential constituent of the diet in spite of what many practitioners say against it, for the young and healthy child is continually using his muscles during his waking hours. The best form of starch is potato, baked or steamed in its skin and taken with butter, this in itself forming a very useful and balanced meal. The next in grade are wholewheat grains, and all starchy products given to the children should be derived from this source. The use of white flour products, which are responsible for many of the troubles of the present day, are never advised and children should be brought up in an atmosphere in which this form of cereal is never regarded as a balanced food.

At least half, if not more, of the daily diet of the child should consist of uncooked foods, composed of fruit and vegetables such as green salads, fresh and dried fruit (the latter being soaked in water only), dates and nuts. Many children have been reared on this diet alone and have attained perfect health, without the addition of any other form of fuel, but modern dietetics seem to point out that additional foods are required by most children in the form of whole grains and dairy produce, namely milk, egg and cheese. The strict vegetarian will not agree to the latter proteins but, having passed though an additional process of vitalization in the animal, they contain more positive material than is commonly found in vegetable building foods and, in my opinion, may be used sparingly in order that their beneficial qualities may be obtained.

HOW MUCH FOOD?

Parents often ask about the quantity of food to give a child, but it is not possible to state this in exact form because children vary so greatly. Teach the child to masticate food, do not force him to eat when he is not inclined and the child will decide the quantities. In this respect there is some room for a piece of advice sometimes given, namely, to allow the child to choose the food he likes on the table and to eat it first. This allows the natural dictates to determine the food and it also prevents the child eating through the meal until the desired food is reached, a method which leads to overeating and indigestion.

Many children will benefit in health by being given a

separate table on which only foods suitable for health building are placed. If the child eats at all, he is getting good food, and if he does not, it is a sign that the body is not ready for food and no coaxing should be tried. Weakly children gradually develop an appetite under this method and it is interesting to note that often the best results are obtained in cases of poor appetite by placing such children on a fast of one or two days, or by giving nothing but fruit for that period. An increase in appetite is then noted and the child may regain his desire for food for quite a period; but if lost again, recourse should be made to fasting, or fruit.

Trying to feed up a child who has no appetite is a most dangerous practice and leads, in many cases, to serious illness. The natural desires of the body are being thwarted and the reaction is usually an illness which, to save the child, will actually prevent eating. Again and again it must be repeated that when there is no appetite the child must not be fed.

SUGGESTED DIET FOR OLDER CHILDREN

On rising, a glass of fruit juice and water should be taken.

Breakfast Wholewheat cereal or bran with a little milk; Dried fruit such as prunes, figs or raisins; One slice of toast, glass of milk.

or

Fresh acid fruit and dried fruit; Glass of milk; Lightly cooked egg occasionally.

Lunch Cottage cheese or small portions of nut dish or vegetarian savoury with steamed vegetables and baked potatoes. Fruit or whole rice pudding or steamed brown flour and dried fruit pudding.

Tea Cup of soup; Wholewheat toast or dried fruit; Small amount of salad, cup of milk.